An A-Z of Extraordinary Extinct Creatures

Jill Michelle Smith

and

Jennifer Watson

A

Archie the
archaeopteryx

Pronounced: *ar-key-op-ter-ix*

Extinct: 147 million years ago   Size: 50 centimetres long

With sharp, clawed wings and a toothy beak,
Archie swooped from Jurassic peaks.
A seagull-sized reptile hungry for lunch,
Of shimmering insects to gulp and crunch.
His famous fossil helped spread the word,
Dinosaurs were ancestors of birds!

Basil the
basilosaurus

Pronounced: *ba-sill-oh-saw-rus*

Extinct: 34 million years ago   Size: 18 metres long

Basil was massive with a sea serpent's motion,
Who hunted down fish in the Eocene ocean.
His body was long and so was his nose,
With small back paddles and front elbows.
Although called "saurus", that's just a tall tale,
In fact, he was an ancient whale!

Callum the

chalicotherium

Pronounced: *ka-lih-co-theer-ee-um*

Extinct: 5 million years ago   Size: 3 metres tall

Callum was such a bizarre-looking creature,
A horse, a bear, a gorilla in features!
With extra long arms, he walked on his knuckles,
And his stout back legs were taut with muscles.
He stretched curvy claws for leaves in treetops,
A giant mammal of the Miocene epoch.

Dotty the

dodo

Pronounced: *doh-doh*

Extinct: 1681　　　Size: 1 metre tall

Everyone's heard of poor Dotty the Dodo,
Who lived in Mauritius, a land of volcanoes.
When sailors discovered her island one day,
Her short, stubby wings couldn't fly her away.
Clumsy and plump and stuck on the ground,
There was nowhere to hide without being found!

Erik the europasaurus

Pronounced: *yoo-roh-pah-saw-rus*

Extinct: 151 million years ago   Size: 6 metres long

For a sauropod, Erik was small,
Yet still the size of a buffalo bull!
His long, lanky neck could stretch high into trees,
To guzzle and gobble on all of the leaves.
Through Jurassic Europe he would tour,
Along with his herd of dinosaurs.

F

Felicity the
falcarius

Pronounced: *fal-care-ree-us*

Extinct: 126 million years ago   Size: 4 metres long

Felicity was the strangest thing,
With feathers on her dinosaur skin.
She had taloned hands to snatch and fight,
And lots of teeth with which to bite.
But, believe it or not, this Cretaceous beast,
Only ate herbivorous feasts!

Gloria the
glossotherium

Pronounced: *gloss-oh-theer-ee-um*

Extinct: 6,000 years ago   Size: 4 metres tall

We all think sloths are cute and furry,
But Gloria was big and burly!
High on her mighty back legs she rose,
The size of a car from tail to nose.
With huge, rugged claws to grab and grip,
And a long, licking tongue to reach plants to pick.

H

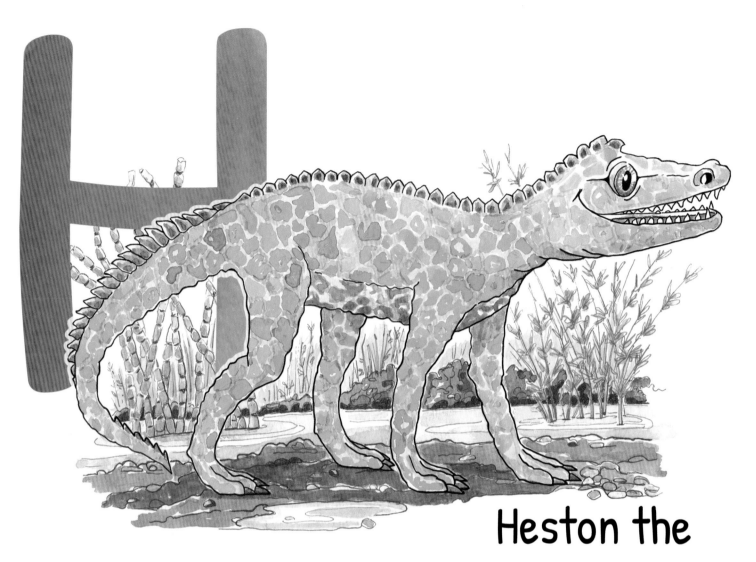

Heston the

hesperosuchus

Pronounced: *hess-per-oh-sook-us*

Extinct: 220 million years ago   Size: 1.5 metres long

Despite his crocodilian form,
Heston's blood was probably warm.
He was speedy on four legs, on two even faster,
So lizards and bugs really had to scarper!
He lived near Triassic swamps and streams,
Where he lurked in the murky mud and steam.

Isla the

iguanodon

Pronounced: *ig-wan-oh-don*

Extinct: 110 million years ago   Size: 10 metres long

Two hundred years ago, when Isla's fossils were uncovered,
She was one of the first dinosaurs to ever be discovered.
She had a tough, toothless beak and a sharp thumb bone,
Which at first was thought to be a horn on her nose.
In truth, her thumb spikes helped her fight off brutes,
And, when she was hungry, she could slice open fruits!

J

Josie the
josephoartigasia

Pronounced: *ho-say-foe-ar-tig-ah-see-ah*

Extinct: 2 million years ago   Size: 3 metres long

Although she looked like a guinea pig,
Josie was immensely big!
Through roots and shoots she'd chomp and gnaw,
A gigantic rodent herbivore.
Across Pliocene wetlands she'd splash and kick,
Kept warm by her fur, spotted and thick.

K

Kenny the
kelenken

Pronounced: *Kell-en-ken*

Extinct: 15 million years ago   Size: 3 metres tall

Kenny was a fast, flightless predator,
Who'd snatch and catch any prey he saw.
With short forelimbs like a tyrannosaurus,
And a deadly beak that was enormous.
Fearsome and frightful as he screeched and swerved,
No wonder he's called a "terror bird"!

Lyla the
lystrosaurus

Pronounced: *list-roh-saw-rus*

Extinct: 247 million years ago   Size: 2 metres long

Before the first ever dinosaur's birth,
Creatures like Lyla roamed the Earth.
She was a Permian species of therapsid,
Who looked a bit like a lizard, a bit like a pig!
Her strong, burrowing legs could dig very deep,
To make a safe place to hide and sleep.

Manu the moa

Pronounced: *moh-ah*

Extinct: 1445   Size: 3.7 metres tall

Hatched from an egg the size of a football,
Manu was a bird who had no wings at all!
With a gangly neck and legs like tree trunks,
He could easily stretch for shrubs to munch.
Across New Zealand he strutted and paced,
Leaving fossilised footprints that were never erased.

N

Nadia the
nodosaur

Pronounced: *nod-oh-saw*

Extinct: 110 million years ago   Size: 5.5 metres long

Nadia's armour of spikes and scales,
Covered her body from head to tail.
She strode boldly across the Cretaceous landscape,
Until one day she fell in a lake!
So tough and robust, that when dug from the ground,
She was the best preserved fossil to ever be found.

Olive the

oxalaia

Pronounced: *ox-ah-lay-ee-ah*

Extinct: 93 million years ago   Size: 14 metres long

Olive was the size of a double-decker bus,
And weighed twice as much as a hippopotamus.
A huge spinosaurus with very sharp claws,
And lots of teeth in her alligator jaws.
This aquatic dinosaur had a sail on her back,
So when hunting in water, she could snap a snack!

P

Percy the

plesiosaur

Pronounced: *plee-see-uh-saw*

Extinct: 66 million years ago   Size: 10 metres long

Alive at the time of the dinosaurs,
Were large sea reptiles called plesiosaurs.
Percy had a sinuous neck and tail,
With four streamlined flippers to splash and sail.
In deep, dark waters he did prosper,
Could he be the Loch Ness Monster?

Q

Quentin the
quetzalcoatlus

Pronounced: *kwet-zal-co-at-lus*

Extinct: 66 million years ago   Size: 11 metres long

Quentin ruled the Cretaceous skies,
He was the largest creature to ever fly.
Towering like a giraffe, with a vastly long neck,
And a gargantuan beak with which to peck.
Over the cliffs he'd swoop and soar,
A truly magnificent pterosaur!

R

Remi the
remingtonocetus

Pronounced: *rem-ing-ton-oh-see-tuss*

Extinct: 45 million years ago   Size: 3 metres long

Remi was a mammal who lived on the shore,
With an otter-like tail and four webbed paws.
From there she returned to the Eocene sea,
Where eventually an ancestor of whales she'd be.
Her spectacular hearing and keen sense of smell,
Made her an excellent hunter of fish as well!

Sampson the
smilodon

Pronounced: *smy-loh-don*

Extinct: 10,000 years ago   Size: 2.5 metres long

Camouflaged and creeping on broad, padded paws,
Sampson had the strongest of all feline jaws.
With sabre-like teeth, so long and sharp,
He would put fear in the bravest heart!
Stalking with stealth through his Pleistocene habitat,
The greatest, most powerful prehistoric cat.

Thora the

thylacine

Pronounced: *thy-la-seen*

Extinct: 1936   Size: 1.6 metres long

Through Tasmanian grasses, Thora would sneak,
Her lean, stripy body so smooth and sleek.
She looked a bit like a dog, but with tiger stripes,
And a pouch for her baby to hide out of sight!
But sadly when settlers from Europe arrived,
This unusual marsupial did not survive.

Unwin the
uintatherium

Pronounced: *win-tah-theer-ee-um*

Extinct: 40 million years ago   Size: 4 metres long

Although Unwin looked rather like a rhinoceros,
His features were certainly far more preposterous.
He meandered in marshland, submersing his head,
So his teeth could plough plants from the green riverbed.
But unlike most mammals, his skull was concave,
So he only had space for a very small brain!

Vernon the
ventastega

Pronounced: *ven-tah-steh-gah*

Extinct: 359 million years ago   Size: 1 metre long

Vernon was a stout, slimy tetrapod,
Who looked half like a newt, half like a frog!
He had pointy teeth for catching his dinner,
A fish from the lake or a snail from the river.
He waddled along the Devonian shores,
In a time long before the dinosaurs.

Wally the woolly mammoth

Pronounced: *wu-lee ma-muhth*

Extinct: 4,000 years ago   Size: 4 metres tall

Wally would plod far across frozen wastes,
Encouraging his herd to keep up and make haste.
With thick, shaggy fur in shades red, blonde and brown,
He would forage through snow for food on the ground.
He had huge, curling tusks and an impressive height,
So with primitive man he could put up a fight!

Xena the
xenoceratops

Pronounced: *zen-oh-sare-ah-tops*

Extinct: 78 million years ago   Size: 6 metres long

A prehistoric beast who polished off plants,
Xena was the size of a modern elephant.
Her decorated head had horns and frills,
With a stiff, sharp beak like a turtle's bill.
It's easy to see why her species' name translates,
As the perfect description; "alien horned face"!

Yasmin the
yinlong

Pronounced: *Yin-long*

Extinct: 157 million years ago   Size: 1.2 metres long

Behind ferny fronds, little Yasmin would hide,
As huge, toothy predators came stomping by!
With three-fingered forelimbs, on her hind legs she'd trot,
A surprising relation of the triceratops.
She cautiously crept through Jurassic bracken,
And her Chinese name means "hidden dragon".

Ziggy the
zygomaturus

Pronounced: *zy-go-mat-yur-us*

Extinct: 45,000 years ago   Size: 2.5 metres long

Ziggy liked munching reeds from the river,
Snuffling them out to have for her dinner.
A giant marsupial, who lumbered along,
Like a weighty wombat, but more sturdy and strong!
She had a teddy bear face with a bulbous nose,
And lived in Australia a long time ago.

Discover the extraordinary
extinct emporium...

dodoanddinosaur.com

An **A-Z** of
Extraordinary Extinct
Creatures

First published in the UK in 2021

Text copyright © 2021 Jill Michelle Smith and Jennifer Watson
Illustrations copyright © 2021 Jill Michelle Smith
Copyright © 2021 Dodo and Dinosaur

Written by Jill Michelle Smith and Jennifer Watson
Illustrated by Jill Michelle Smith
Designed by Jennifer Watson

Printed on 100% sustainably sourced, Carbon Balanced paper
by Barnwell Print Ltd in association with World Land Trust.
Helping to preserve critically threatened tropical rainforests.

WORLD
LAND
TRUST™

www.carbonbalancedprinter.com
Barnwell Print - Reg. 2102
CBP004796